D0538443

TWISTED TREATS

Desserts with Unexpected Ingredients

by HEATHER KIM

COMPASS POINT BOOKS
a capstone imprint

Butter Pound Cake with Sriracha Icing **10**

Flamin' Hot Cheetos® Ice Cream Sandwiches **12**

Corn Bread with Honey Mustard Butter **16**

Eggy Custard Dim Sum **22**

Leches Cake with Malted Milk Whipped Cream and Dulce De Leche **26**

Coconut Mochi Cake with Coconut Sesame Pecan Icing **30**

Cracker Jack® Nut Brittle **38**

Dessert Pizza with Funyuns® Topping **40**

Peanut Fritos® Candy **44**

Strawberry Biscuits with Chicken Skin Candy 18

Carrot Cake Truffles with Cool Ranch Doritos® Sugar 34

TABLE OF CONTENTS

NOT YOUR MOM'S DESSERTS

You love desserts. You love creating them, or you at least love eating them. But you're tired of the same ol', same ol'? So how about adding a hot and spicy, or a sweet and sassy, surprise to your cakes and candies?

Try these recipes with unexpected ingredients. From Sriracha sauce-covered cake to chicken skin candy to hot Cheetos® ice cream and even Cool Ranch Doritos® frosting, these unusual ingredients are not what you'd expect! Yes, they might sound bizarre, but with a little adventurousness you will find that these quirky recipes yield delicious results. They're great for sharing with friends, taking to a party, or saving all for yourself.

PLAYING IT SAFE

Measuring precisely and following the directions should bring great results and fine desserts. Don't ruin your success by having an accident in the kitchen. Follow these safety precautions as you work:

Always wash your hands before you begin baking, if you spill, and after touching raw eggs.

Use caution when handling sharp objects. Ask for an adult's help when a recipe calls for chopping, slicing, or cutting. Hold the knife's handle firmly when cutting and keep fingers away from the blade.

Also be careful when working near hot surfaces. It's best to have an adult help when operating the stovetop and oven at high temperatures. When using saucepans, turn the handles toward the center of the stove to avoid bumping a handle and spilling. Always wear oven mitts or pot holders to take hot baking sheets or cake pans out of the oven.

Spills and messes are bound to happen in the kitchen. Wipe up messes with paper towels or a damp kitchen towel. Keep your countertop clean and dry.

MIX IT UP

Your time in the kitchen will go more smoothly if you prepare and plan ahead. Read through each recipe before you begin. Some recipes may require several hours before they are ready. Gather any supplies you need ahead of time. If you're not sure how to do something that a recipe asks, check this list.

mixing bowl

electric mixer

food processor

mixing spoon

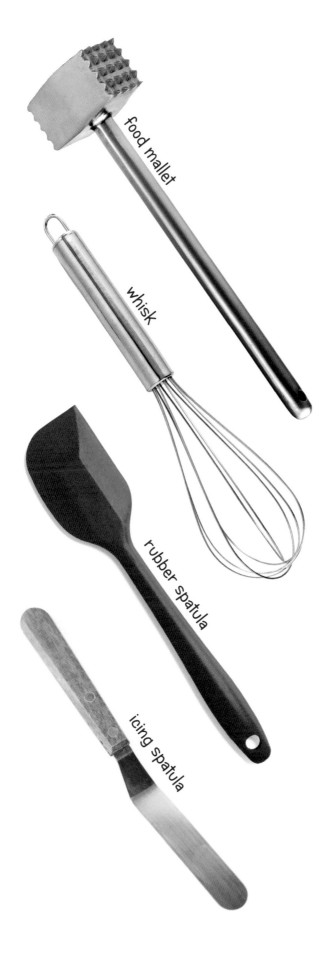

food mallet

whisk

rubber spatula

icing spatula

BEAT IT
Create a smooth, creamy mixture by stirring briskly, using a spoon, whisk, or mixer.

CREAM IT
Vigorously beat and stir ingredients. The result? Creamy, fluffy smoothness.

DIVIDE IT
If an ingredient is "divided" or "separated," you'll only use part of the total amount at one time.

WHIP IT
Add air and volume to a mixture using a whisk or mixer.

WHISK IT
Use a whisk to combine ingredients using a side-to-side motion. If you don't have a whisk, use two forks.

FEELING HOT

Time to spice it up! A little bit of heat can be an unexpectedly delicious contrast to cakes and ice cream. These fiery sweets are guaranteed to heat up your dessert game.

BUTTER POUND CAKE
WITH SRIRACHA ICING

Pound cake gets its name from traditional versions of the recipe that call for a pound of flour, a pound of butter (you read that right!), a pound of sugar, and a pound of eggs. This recipe doesn't require quite that much of each ingredient. Whatever the ingredients, you can make this for any occasion. The sriracha icing gives it a spicy twist!

CAKE

2 1/3 cups all-purpose flour

1 1/2 teaspoons baking powder

1 teaspoon salt

1 3/4 cups granulated sugar

1 1/4 cups butter

2 large egg yolks

3 large eggs

2/3 cup heavy cream

1 1/2 teaspoons vanilla extract

1 Make sure your ingredients are at room temperature before you begin. Preheat oven to 350°F. Butter a Bundt cake mold and dust with flour.

2 In a medium bowl, whisk all the dry ingredients together (flour, baking powder, and salt). Set aside.

3 In a large bowl, whip the butter and sugar together until lightly golden and fluffy. Scrape down the sides. Add the eggs and yolks, one at a time, scraping down the bowl after each addition.

4 Add half of the dry mixture and half of the heavy cream. Mix. Scrape. Repeat.

5 Stir in vanilla until just combined. Do not overmix.

6 Bake 30 to 45 minutes or until a toothpick comes out cleanly from the center. The time will depend on the size and shape of your Bundt mold.

ICING

1 8-ounce package cream cheese

1 stick butter

4 cups powdered sugar

sriracha, to taste

1 Whip together the cream cheese and butter. Then slowly add powdered sugar until fluffy.

2 Squeeze in preferred amount of sriracha or drizzle on top after cake is assembled.

TO ASSEMBLE

Flip cooled Bundt cake onto a serving platter. Cut into slices and add a dollop of icing.

– SASSY TIP –

To separate egg yolks from the whites, crack open the egg. Let the whites fall into a bowl below. Move the yolk back and forth between the two halves of the cracked egg until all the white has fallen below. Save the whites for another use. Remember to always wash your hands with soap and water after touching raw eggs.

FLAMIN' HOT CHEETOS® ICE CREAM SANDWICHES

A little sweet and a little spice, these ice cream sandwiches are everything nice! The Flamin' Hot Cheetos® flavored cookies and ganache are a perfect pair for cold ice cream. Both hot and cold, it's the best of both worlds.

FLAMIN' HOT CHEETOS® SUGAR

granulated sugar

1 bag Flamin' Hot Cheetos®, ground

TO MAKE

Mix two parts sugar to one part Flamin' Hot Cheetos®.

SUGAR COOKIES

2 cups all-purpose flour

1 cup Flamin' Hot Cheetos®, ground

2 teaspoons baking powder

1/2 cup butter

1 cup granulated sugar

2 eggs

1 **Preheat oven to 350°F.**

2 **In a medium bowl, mix the flour, Flamin' Hot Cheetos®, and baking powder. Set aside.**

3 **In a separate bowl, cream the butter and sugar until pale yellow and fluffy. Add eggs, one by one, until completely combined. Add the dry ingredients and combine.**

4 **Scoop dough into a large ball and roll into Flamin' Hot Cheetos® sugar. Then press onto a parchment- or Silpat®-lined baking sheet until cookies are about 0.5 inch (1.3 cm) thick.**

5 **Bake for about 15 minutes, turning halfway through. Cookies are done when fluorescent red in color and medium-soft to the touch.**

GANACHE

2 ounces Flamin' Hot Cheetos®, food processed into fine crumbs

1 cup heavy cream

1 cup white chocolate chips

1 **In a medium saucepan, set over medium-high heat, stir Flamin' Hot Cheetos® into heavy cream. Bring the liquid to a boil, then remove the pan from the heat.**

2 **Mix and melt white chocolate in. Set aside to cool.**

TO ASSEMBLE

1 **Choose two cookies of similar shape and size. Place one cookie facedown on a plate.**

2 **Scoop ice cream on top of cookie, spoon ganache over ice cream, and top with second cookie.**

SASSY FACT
Made for nonstick cooking, a Silpat® silicone rubber mat is great when working with sticky stuff, like gooey batter, taffy, caramel, or dough.

A SIDE OF DESSERT

You might think ingredients like honey mustard and chicken go better in dinner than dessert. Not in these recipes! These dishes are filled with flavors from both the main course and dessert. What more could you ask for?

CORN BREAD WITH HONEY MUSTARD BUTTER

Craving a moist, crackly topped slice of corn bread? This simple yet delicious treat is easy to make and can be served for breakfast, lunch, or dinner. Don't forget the buttery, tangy mustard sauce on top!

CORN BREAD

1 cup cornmeal

3 cups all-purpose flour

1 1/3 cups granulated sugar

2 tablespoons baking powder

1 teaspoon salt

2/3 cup vegetable oil

1/3 cup melted butter

2 tablespoons honey

4 eggs, beaten

2 1/2 cups whole milk

HONEY MUSTARD BUTTER

1 stick butter, room temp

1 tablespoon honey

1 teaspoon dry mustard

1/2 teaspoon salt

1 Preheat oven to 350°F. Butter
a 9- x 13-inch (23- x 33-cm) baking
dish and set aside.

2 In a large mixing bowl, whisk together
the dry ingredients (cornmeal, flour,
sugar, baking powder, and salt).

3 Add the oil, butter, honey, eggs, and
milk. Stir just until moist.

4 Pour batter in the prepared baking
dish. Bake for about 45 minutes, or
until a toothpick comes out clean and
corn bread is golden-brown.

5 Meanwhile, combine honey mustard
butter ingredients in a food processor
and pulse until combined.

6 Serve corn bread hot out of the oven
with butter melting on top.

STRAWBERRY BISCUITS WITH CHICKEN SKIN CANDY

Eat them for dessert, or have them as a side with your dinner. Either way, don't chicken out— try these delicious biscuits with their to-die-for toppings!

BISCUITS

2 cups all-purpose flour

2 teaspoons salt

1 tablespoon baking powder

1 tablespoon granulated sugar

1 1/2 cups heavy cream

sugar, for sprinkling (optional)

1. Preheat oven to 425°F. Line a cookie sheet with a Silpat® mat or parchment paper.

2. In a large bowl, mix all dry ingredients (flour, salt, baking powder, and sugar). Add cream and mix.

3. Using an ice cream scoop or a large cookie scoop, plop mounds of dough onto the prepped sheet. Flatten with your palm until they are about 1 inch (2.5 cm) thick. Sprinkle with sugar, if desired.

4. Bake for about 15 minutes or until golden. Serve hot.

JAM

1 cup strawberries, pureed

1 cup granulated sugar, divided

1/4 cup apple cider vinegar

1 teaspoon pectin, powdered

1 cup strawberries, diced

salt and black pepper, to taste

1. In a medium saucepan, heat the pureed strawberries, 1/2 cup of the sugar, and the vinegar until hot.

2. Stir in the powdered pectin and the other 1/2 cup of sugar. While whisking, heat to boil, then simmer for about 3 minutes. Remove from heat.

3. When cooled to room temp, add the diced strawberries and salt and black pepper. Whisk together. Refrigerate until needed.

Recipe continues on next page.

ICING

2 cups powdered sugar

1 tablespoon butter, softened

1/2 teaspoon salt

1/2 teaspoon vanilla extract

1/2 cup maple syrup

TO MAKE

In a medium bowl, stir all ingredients together until spreadable.

CHICKEN SKIN CANDY

1/2 pound chicken skin (about 3 thighs' worth)

granulated sugar

kosher salt

freshly ground pepper, to taste

1 Preheat oven to 350°F. Trim excess fat from chicken skin. Cut into 3-inch (7.6-cm) pieces.

2 Coat skin in sugar. Sprinkle with salt and pepper.

3 Flatten, flesh-side down, on a baking sheet lined with parchment paper. Top with another sheet of parchment and a baking sheet to keep skin from curling.

4 Bake until browned and crispy, about 1 hour.

5 Remove top baking sheet and paper. Let cool for 10 minutes.

TO ASSEMBLE:

1 Split hot biscuits in half.

2 Scoop strawberry filling onto the bottom half of a biscuit. Replace the top half. Serve with a dollop of maple icing and chicken skin candy.

– SASSY TIP –
Bake chicken skin candy ahead of time. Store in an airtight container in the fridge for 1 to 2 days.

EGGY CUSTARD DIM SUM

Egg tarts, similar to English custard tarts, are a common pastry in Hong Kong, Macau, and other parts of China. These bite-sized egg yolk custard treats, nestled in a flaky, tender crust, are dim sum staples. Eat them quickly—they're best when hot and fresh from the oven!

1 package puff pastry dough

1 egg, beaten

FILLING

1/2 cup granulated sugar

1/2 teaspoon cornstarch

1/2 teaspoon salt

3/4 cup whole milk

2/3 cup heavy cream

8 large yolks (see page 11)

1 teaspoon vanilla extract

1 Preheat oven to 375°F. Lightly grease a 12-cup muffin tin.

2 Cut puff pastry into squares, pressing them firmly into the muffin tin.

3 In a medium bowl, whisk together the sugar, cornstarch, and salt. Add the milk, cream, yolks, and vanilla and whisk again until combined.

4 Fill each cup with custard to about 0.2 inch (0.5 cm) from the top of the crust. Brush edges with an egg wash. Bake until crust is golden and custard is just set, about 20 minutes.

5 Cool in the pan for 15 minutes. Move to a wire rack to cool completely.

– SASSY TIP –
Egg washes help give crusts a more golden finish. To make an egg wash, beat an egg and mix with a little water, milk, or cream. Simply brush onto the crust with a pastry brush.

SASSY FACT
What is dim sum? Put simply, it's a traditional Chinese food served in small portions and shared. Although it can be anything really (such as tiny bites of chicken or pork), dumplings served in steamer baskets are dim sum faves!

EXQUISITELY SWEET CAKES

Cakes are great for special occasions. But why save them for birthdays and graduations when you can make one now? These sugary sweet cakes can (and should!) be eaten at any time. Drenched in drizzle and crowned with over-the-top icing, you won't be able to stop at one slice!

LECHES CAKE WITH MALTED MILK WHIPPED CREAM AND DULCE DE LECHE

Just like traditional *tres leches* cakes, this cake is soaked in three kinds of milk. Then we add whipped cream on top. And since you can never be too overachieving with your desserts, it is served with a sweet sauce.

CAKE

2 cups cake flour, plus extra for the pan

1 teaspoon baking powder

1 teaspoon salt

8 tablespoons butter, room temperature

3 tablespoons granulated sugar

5 eggs

1 1/2 teaspoons vanilla extract

GLAZE

1 (12-ounce) can evaporated milk

1 (14-ounce) can sweetened condensed milk

1 cup half-and-half

1 Preheat oven to 350°F. Butter or spray a 13- x 9-inch (33- x 23-cm) baking pan.

2 Whisk together the cake flour, baking powder, and salt in a medium bowl.

3 In a large mixing bowl, beat butter on medium speed of a stand mixer until fluffy, about 1 minute.

4 Drop the speed to low, and slowly add the sugar during the next minute. Stop and scrape down sides of the bowl.

5 Crack in the eggs, one by one, mixing until each is completely combined.

6 Add the vanilla and mix to combine.

7 Add flour mixture to the batter in three batches, mixing until just combined. Do not overmix.

8 Transfer batter to the prepared baking pan and spread evenly. (The amount of batter may appear pretty small, but don't worry!)

9 Bake for 20 minutes, turning halfway through, until cake is golden.

10 Using a skewer or fork, poke small holes across top of cake. Set aside, allowing to cool completely.

11 For glaze, whisk the evaporated milk, sweetened condensed milk, and half-and-half in a medium bowl until combined.

12 Pour glaze mixture over cooled cake. Cover with plastic wrap and refrigerate overnight.

Recipe continues on next page.

– SASSY TIP –
Here's a really easy way to make this recipe: Buy a box of yellow or white cake mix, and follow the instructions on the box. Assemble with glaze from this recipe, 1 tub of whipped topping, and a squeeze bottle of dulce de leche topping.

WHIPPED CREAM

2 cups heavy cream

1 cup granulated sugar

1 teaspoon vanilla extract

3/4 cup vanilla malted milk

1 Combine the cream, sugar, vanilla, and malted milk into a cold mixing bowl.

2 With an electric mixer, whisk ingredients on high speed until fluffy, about 1 minute.

DULCE DE LECHE DRIZZLE

14-ounce can sweetened condensed milk

1 Peel the label off the unopened can of sweetened condensed milk and discard. Place the can in a medium saucepan, and cover completely with water.

2 Boil for about 3 hours, replenishing water as needed to keep can fully submerged.

3 Remove from heat. Let the can cool to room temperature.

4 Open can.

TO ASSEMBLE

1 Using an icing spatula or butter knife, frost the *cinco leches* cake with malted milk whipped cream.

2 Drizzle dulce de leche on plate and place cake on top. Sprinkle with a pinch of salt and top with fresh berries, if desired.

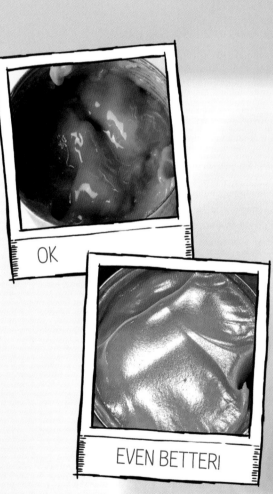

OK

EVEN BETTER!

– SASSY TIP –

Longer or shorter cooking times could result in color or consistency variations. Experiment and find the dulce de leche that tastes best to you.

COCONUT MOCHI CAKE with COCONUT SESAME PECAN ICING

In Japan mochi is a small, round cake made with rice flour. But why stop at small when you can make it full-sized? Then take it to the next level of unexpected with coconut sesame pecan icing.

CAKE

4 cups sweetened rice flour

1 tablespoon baking powder

3 cups granulated sugar

1/2 cup melted butter

4 eggs

1 (12-ounce) can coconut milk, full fat

1 (12-ounce) can evaporated milk, full fat

1 teaspoon vanilla extract

1/2 teaspoon almond extract

1 teaspoon coconut extract

1/2 teaspoon salt

1 Preheat oven to 350°F. Butter or spray a 13- x 9-inch (33- x 23-cm) baking pan.

2 In a medium bowl, stir together the rice flour, baking powder, and sugar.

3 In a large bowl, stir together all the remaining ingredients. Add dry ingredients and mix until completely combined.

4 Pour this batter into the prepared baking dish, spreading evenly.

5 Bake about 1 hour or until center is golden and all edges are golden-brown.

ICING

2/3 cup sugar

2/3 cup evaporated milk

2 egg yolks (see page 11)

6 tablespoons butter

1/2 teaspoon vanilla extract

1/2 teaspoon salt

1 cup coconut flakes

1 cup pecans, chopped

1/4 cup toasted sesame seeds

1 In a large saucepan over low heat, whisk the sugar, evaporated milk, egg yolks, butter, and vanilla, until yolks thicken up.

2 Remove from heat and stir in the salt, coconut, pecans, and sesame seeds.

TO ASSEMBLE

1 Using an icing spatula or butter knife, frost coconut mochi cake with coconut sesame pecan icing.

2 Slice and serve it warm.

SASSY FACT
Mochi ice cream is becoming a popular snack around the world. This heavenly snack wraps mochi dough around a ball of ice cream.

JUNK FOOD AISLE

Junk food is best straight out of the package, right? Think again! Whether you're having some friends over or just craving a guilty pleasure, making desserts with junk food aisle favorites opens up a whole new world of possibilities.

CARROT CAKE TRUFFLES WITH COOL RANCH DORITOS® SUGAR

Not a fan of mixing veggies with dessert? Try these carrot cake truffles and you just might change your mind! These tiny bites are full of flavor and topped with a sweet frosting to make a perfectly decadent sassy sweet.

CAKE

1 1/2 cups all-purpose flour

1 cup granulated sugar

1 1/2 teaspoons baking soda

1 teaspoon baking powder

2 teaspoons cinnamon

1/2 teaspoon ground cloves

1/2 teaspoon nutmeg

1/2 teaspoon ginger, grated

1/2 teaspoon salt

2/3 cup vegetable oil

3 large eggs, beaten

1 1/2 cups carrots, peeled and finely grated

1 Preheat oven to 350°F.

2 In a large bowl, whisk together the flour, sugar, baking soda, baking powder, spices, and salt until completely combined.

3 Stir in oil and beaten eggs. Add the carrots and stir again until ingredients are combined.

4 With a rubber spatula, scrape the batter into a 13- x 9-inch (33- x 23-cm) cake pan, spreading evenly.

5 Bake for 30 to 35 minutes or until a toothpick inserted into the center comes out clean.

6 Allow to cool. Cut it into large cubes.

7 Place cubes into a food processor and pulse until cake is completely crumbled. Or smash with your hands.

Recipe continues on next page. ⟶

FROSTING

4 ounces cream cheese, room temperature

1/2 cup butter, room temperature

2 cups powdered sugar

1 teaspoon vanilla extract

1/2 teaspoon salt

1 **In a large mixing bowl, whip the cream cheese and butter until light and fluffy. Scrape down the sides of the bowl with a rubber spatula.**

2 **Slowly add the powdered sugar, then vanilla and salt, whipping until fluffy. Scrape down the sides of the bowl again.**

COOL RANCH DORITOS® SUGAR

1 cup Cool Ranch Doritos®, crumbled

1/2 cup granulated sugar

TO MAKE

In a tiny bowl, mix crumbled
Cool Ranch Doritos® and sugar
until combined.

TO ASSEMBLE

1 Fold carrot cake crumbles into frosting
mixture with a rubber spatula, blending
until well-incorporated.

2 Using a small scoop or spoon, scoop
cake mixture into truffle balls.

3 Gently roll truffle balls, one by one, in
Cool Ranch Doritos® sugar, coating
until deliciously dusted.

CRACKER JACK® NUT BRITTLE

Buy yourself some peanuts and Cracker Jack®, make this nut brittle, and there's no going back! Sugary, buttery, and crunchy, it's a treat everyone will think is a winner.

INGREDIENTS

1 cup butter

1 cup granulated sugar

1 cup brown sugar

1 cup corn syrup

1 teaspoon vanilla extract

1/2 teaspoon baking soda

1 pound peanuts, dry roasted and salted

1 box Cracker Jack®

– SASSY TIP –
No Cracker Jack®? No problem!
Replace with caramel corn or hard
cereals, such as Cap'n Crunch®,
Kix®, or some fall-festive
Apple Jacks®.

1 **Preheat oven to 250°F. Line a sheet pan with a Silpat® mat or parchment paper.**

2 **In a medium saucepan, boil the butter, sugars, and corn syrup for 5 minutes.**

3 **Remove from heat. Stir in the vanilla extract and baking soda. Then stir in the peanuts. Do not overstir.**

4 **Spread onto the prepped sheet. Bake for 45 minutes, stirring every 15 minutes or so.**

5 **Remove the sheet from the oven and immediately stir in Cracker Jack®.**

6 **Cool completely and then smash into pieces with a mallet or your fist.**

DESSERT PIZZA WITH FUNYUNS® TOPPING

What do you want on your pizza? Pepperoni? Mushrooms? Funyuns®? Wait a minute! Pizza is not just for dinner. It's for dessert too. With a cookie crust, frosting sauce, and a butterscotch Funyuns® topping, it's sure to be a crowd-pleaser.

SNICKERDOODLE CRUST

2 3/4 cups all-purpose flour

2 teaspoons baking powder

1 teaspoon salt

1/2 cup butter

1 cup granulated sugar

2 eggs

sugar and sprinkles, optional

1 **Preheat oven to 350°F.**

2 **Line a pizza pan with parchment paper and grease with nonstick cooking spray.**

3 **Mix the flour, baking powder, and salt in a medium bowl. Set aside.**

4 **In a separate bowl, cream the butter and sugar until pale yellow and fluffy. Crack in the eggs, one by one. Mix until totally combined.**

5 **Combine dry and wet ingredients.**

6 **Press cookie dough into a large, round pizza shape, until approximately 0.5 inch (1.3 cm) thick.**

7 **Sprinkle with sugar and sprinkles, if desired.**

8 **Bake for 20 minutes, turning halfway through baking time. Cookie is done when pale yellow and firm to touch in the center.**

9 **Let cool completely.**

Recipe continues on next page. →

FROSTING

1 2/3 cups white chocolate chips

1 cup sour cream

1/2 teaspoon vanilla extract

1 In a medium saucepan over low heat, melt white chocolate chips, stirring often.

2 When creamy and fully melted, take off heat. Stir in the sour cream and vanilla.

BUTTERSCOTCH FUNYUNS®

12 hard caramel candies

1 medium-sized bag of Funyuns®

1 cup butterscotch chips

2 tablespoons butter

1 In a food processor, pulverize the hard caramel candies into tiny chips and dust. Set aside.

2 Lay out Funyuns® in a single layer on a cookie sheet.

3 Melt butterscotch and butter in microwave at 15-second intervals.

4 Dip Funyuns® facedown into butterscotch and then immediately into candy dust.

TO ASSEMBLE

1 **Spread frosting across pizza.**

2 **Place butterscotch Funyuns® on top.
   Slice and serve.**

– SASSY TIP –
Don't limit yourself to Butterscotch Funyuns®! Get creative. Get wild. Top this pizza with whatever you want. Hit up the snack aisle and challenge yourself and your taste buds. Want to top this pizza with Skittles®? Why not! Want beef jerky on your pizza? Go right ahead! Donut? Don't mind if I do!

PEANUT FRITOS® CANDY

Whip up some Peanut Fritos® Candy for a treat that's equal parts salty, crunchy, and sweet. Creamy peanut butter poured over tasty corn chips makes a dessert candy that is unexpectedly delicious. Just be sure to make enough for everyone—your family and friends are going to be begging for more!

INGREDIENTS

10 ounces Fritos®

1 cup salted roasted peanuts

1 cup granulated sugar

1 cup light corn syrup

1 cup creamy peanut butter

1 cup Reese's Pieces®

1 Place Fritos® and peanuts onto a greased or Silpat®-lined 10- x 15-inch (25- x 38-cm) sheet pan.

2 In a medium saucepan, bring the sugar and corn syrup to a boil. Remove from heat. Stir in peanut butter, mixing until smooth.

3 Pour the mixture evenly over chips and nuts. Sprinkle the Reese's Pieces® across top.

4 Let cool to room temperature. Break into pieces.

METRIC CONVERSIONS

The measurements used in this book are imperial units. If you need metric units, check below.

TEMPERATURE

250°F	160°C
350°F	180°C
375°F	190°C
425°F	220°C

VOLUME

1/2 teaspoon	2.5 g or mL
1 teaspoon	5 g or mL
1 tablespoon	15 g or mL
1/4 cup	57 g (dry) or 60 mL (liquid)
1/3 cup	75 g (dry) or 80 mL (liquid)
1/2 cup	114 g (dry) or 125 mL (liquid)
2/3 cup	150 g (dry) or 160 mL (liquid)
3/4 cup	170 g (dry) or 175 mL (liquid)
1 cup	227 g (dry) or 240 mL (liquid)

WEIGHT

2 ounces	57 g
4 ounces	113 g
10 ounces	284 g

READ MORE

Besel, Jen. *Custom Confections: Delicious Desserts You Can Create and Enjoy.* North Mankato, Minn.: Capstone Young Readers, 2015.

Cook, Deanna F. *Baking Class: 50 Fun Recipes Kids Will Love to Bake!* North Adams, Mass.: Storey Publishing, 2017.

Dyer, Janice. *Get into Smart Snacks.* Get-into-It Guides. New York: Crabtree Publishing, 2018.

Huff, Lisa. *Kid Chef Bakes: The Kids Cookbook for Aspiring Bakers.* Berkeley, Calif.: Rockridge Press, 2017.

Jorgensen, Katrina. *Ballpark Eats: Recipes Inspired by America's Baseball Stadiums.* North Mankato, Minn.: Capstone Young Readers, 2016.

INTERNET SITES

Use FactHound to find Internet sites related to this book.

Visit *www.facthound.com*

Just type in 9781543530209 and go.

ABOUT THE AUTHOR

Heather Kim is a pastry chef, painter, and tattoo artist at Minneapolis Tattoo Shop, an all-female owned and operated parlor. Her deliciously unconventional desserts have been praised by the Minneapolis *Star Tribune*, *Minnesota Monthly*, and *Eater*. She lives in Minneapolis with her college sweetheart, Scottie, and their schnauzers, Max and Nietzsche.

Check out all the books in the Sassy Sweets series.

Compass Point Books are published by Capstone
1710 Roe Crest Drive, North Mankato, Minnesota 56003
www.mycapstone.com

Image Credits
Photographs by Capstone Studio: Karon Dubke, except: Shutterstock: Anna Kucherova, 20, Arayabandit, 6 Bottom Left, atdr, 4 Bottom Left, Becky Starsmore, 7 Bottom Middle, Binh Thanh Bui, 41 Top, Diana Taliun, 42 Top Right, Freer, 27, gowithstock, 31, Iakov Filimonov, 6 Top Right, Igors Rusakovs, 42 Bottom Right, Irina Sokolovskaya, 41 Bottom, Michal Schwarz, 4 Middle Left, Sean van Tonder, 6 Bottom Right, VictorH11, 6 Top Left, W Photowork, 7 Bottom, wavebreakmedia, 4 Top Left, Yuliya Gontar, Design Element, 4–5, 46–47

Editorial Credits
Abby Colich, editor; Juliette Peters and Charmaine Whitman, designers; Tracy Cummins, media researcher; Karon Dubke, photographer; Sarah Schuette, photo stylist; Laura Manthe, production specialist

Library of Congress Cataloging-in-Publication Data
Names: Kim, Heather, 1978- author.
Title: Twisted treats : desserts with unexpected ingredients / by Heather Kim.
Description: North Mankato, Minnesota : Compass Point Books, a Capstone imprint, [2019] | Series: Sassy sweets | Audience: Ages 9-11. | Audience: Grades 4 to 6.
Identifiers: LCCN 2018017832l ISBN 9781543530209 (library binding) | ISBN 9781543530254 (ebook pdf)
Subjects: LCSH: Desserts—Juvenile literature. | LCGFT: Cookbooks.
Classification: LCC TX773 .K2264 2019 | DDC 641.86—dc23
LC record available at https://lccn.loc.gov/2018017832

Printed in the United States of America.
PA021